INFO BANK

HISTORY

First published by Miles Kelly Publishing Ltd
Bardfield Centre, Great Bardfield
Essex, CM7 4SL

2 4 6 8 10 9 7 5 3 1

Editor
Isla MacCuish

Designer
Venita Kidwai

Editorial Director
Paula Borton

Art Director
Clare Sleven

Picture Research
Liberty Newton

British Library Cataloguing-in-Publication Data
A catalogue record for this book is available from the British Library

ISBN 1-84236-056-6
Printed in Hong Kong

www.mileskelly.net
info@mileskelly.net

Acknowledgements

The publishers would like to thank the following artists whose work appears in this book:

Nicholas Forder, Terry Gabbey (AFA Ltd), Luigi Galante Studios, Sally Holmes,
Richard Hook (Linden Artists), John James (Temple Rogers), Kevin Maddison, Janos Marffy,
Pete Roberts (Allied Artists), Eric Rowe (Linden Artists), Martin Sanders, Rob Sheffield,
Guy Smith (Mainline Design), Mike Taylor (SGA), Rudi Vizi, Mike White (Temple Rogers).

The publishers would like to thank the following sources for the photographs used in this book:

P40-41 (R) Dover Publications; Page 60-61 (C) Werner Forman/CORBIS;
Page 64-65 (C) Bettman/CORBIS; Page 64-65 (B/R) Archivo Iconografico/CORBIS;
Page 66-67(B/L) Dover Publications; Page 72-73 (C) Hulton-Deutsch Collection/CORBIS;
P76-77 (L) Bettman/CORBIS; P84-85 (L) Lowell Georgia/CORBIS

All other photographs from Miles Kelly archives.

INFO BANK

HISTORY

RICHARD TAMES

Miles Kelly

PUBLISHING

CONTENTS

HISTORICAL ERAS

Ancient Egypt

Civilization, based on writing and city life, began in the great river valleys of Egypt, Iraq, India and China. Created around 3000 BC, Egyptian civilization lasted for 3000 years, surviving long periods of disorder, until it became part of the Roman Empire on the death of Cleopatra.

Ancient Greece

The 300 warring city-states of the Greek world destroyed themselves in the end. However, even their conquerors respected their legacy of medicine, drama, architecture, mathematics, the writing of history and study of politics. Our own alphabet came from ancient Greece.

The Roman Empire

Roman civilization was practical, a world of order shown through good roads, bridges, laws, sanitation and awesome military power. Even after the last emperor was deposed in 476, the legacy of Roman achievements remained an ideal that Europeans aimed to recreate.

Age of Invasions

After 800, a new Christian empire took hold in Europe – modelled on the successes of the Roman empire. During this time Christianity spread west to reclaim Spain and Portugal from Islam and east to save Hungary, Poland and Scandinavia from paganism.

Age of Faiths

Politics and religion remained inseparable. Christian Europe faced unrest within as Catholics fought Protestants and was threatened by Islam spreading to the east. Meanwhile in India, the Mughal emperor Akbar tried to rule Muslims and Hindus in harmony.

Age of Monarchs

Gunpowder gave rulers the power to crush uprisings. Powerful kings and queens, ruled in Spain, France, England and Russia. Further east, the Ming, Ottomans and Mughals ruled empires of even greater splendour with power unchallenged by Parliament or Pope.

A Widening World

Attempting to find a new route to China, Columbus arrived instead in America. Oceans became bridges between continents. The laying of the first Atlantic telegraph cable in 1866 made it possible to communicate with America in seconds.

Age of Steam and Iron

Railways could run seven times as fast as stage coaches, distributing the cloth and other goods produced in factories. Rails, bridges and boats brought people to new lands like the prairies in the US, and kept them in touch through cheap postage and daily newspapers.

Age of Empires

1763 saw Britain dominant in Canada and India; by 1914 its empire was the largest the world had ever seen. Africa, the Caribbean and most of Asia were controlled by rival empires, creating a way forward for trade, migration, missionary work and the spread of technology.

One world

World wars destroyed empires, and new technologies created a communications revolution. Entering the third millennium, the urban lifestyles and the highly developed civilizations that began in the cities of the ancient world have now been adopted worldwide.

HOW TO USE THE SUBJECT LINKS

Navigate your way through this book using the colour-coded lozenges located in the bottom right hand corner of every spread. Flip through the pages, matching colours and sub-headings, and you can compare and contrast themes such as people in power, home life and travel and trade across ten different historical eras.

19-11 AGE OF STEAM & IRON 1779–1850

Mechanized farming
By the mid 19th century steam-powered machinery was being used by the wealthier farmers in Europe and America. Industry also supplied cheap iron tools, clay pipes to drain soils and tiles to replace thatch on roofs.

Steam-powered farming
Linked to the threshing machine, the steam engine could complete the job in a fraction of the time it used to take. Farming was becoming more intensive.

Mixed farming
Many farms both produced crops and raised livestock, rather than specializing in either. This was less risky than relying on a single product which could be wiped out by drought or disease.

Machine workers
While farmers prospered their labourers rarely did. Harvest time meant very long hours but in winter there was often little work, so little pay. Labourers left the land for better jobs in towns or to emigrate overseas. Farmers brought machines to do much of the work fewer...

Sheepshearing
Many farmers had huge flocks of sheep. The wool from their fleeces was always in demand.

FARMERS & FARMING

12-13 ANCIENT EGYPT 3000–30 BC

Gift of the Nile
The Greek historian Herodotus called Egypt 'the gift of the Nile'. Every year, as the mountain snow melted in the south, the world's longest river flooded, leaving a thick layer of mud on both sides of its banks. This made it possible to produce at least two, and often three, crops a year. The main crops were wheat for bread and barley for beer. Flax and cotton were grown to make clothing. The people ate a lot of beans, figs, dates, garlic and salad vegetables.

Raising water
This cheap and simple device called a shaduf used a counterweight of stone or mud to lever up water from one level to the next. It is still in use today.

Rich harvest
All land was, in theory, owned by the pharaoh. The pharaoh looked after his people by setting aside some of each year's grain crop in huge stores, to control distribution. If the harvest failed, this grain could be used to make up the shortfall and prevent famine.

Egypt's lifeline
The Nile held Egypt together. Without the cheap method of transport it provided it would not have been possible for Thebes and Luxor to grow into great cities by relying on food transported over long distances. Reeds growing along the river's banks yielded papyrus on which records of taxes and grain stores were kept.

The Nile Delta
For most of its length the banks of the Nile were fertile for only a few kilometres either side before desert took over. But as the river neared the sea, it fanned out to make a delta 240 km wide. This rich, marshy region was rich in fish and wildfowl to vary the local diet. Marshy areas yielded reeds which were woven to make baskets, ropes, sleeping mats, shoes and even boats.

Irrigation
Egyptian farmers became expert in digging and controlling complex systems of canals, basins, dams and tanks to distribute and store the water of the great river so that it could be used to best effect.

FARMERS & FARMING

Flip the pages and match the corner bars by colour. Make the links between ten different topics.

ANCIENT EGYPT 3000–30 BC

Construction for kings

The pyramids of Egypt were built as tombs for pharaohs (kings) between 2700 BC and 1750 BC. Egypt's fertile soil produced a food surplus which enabled thousands of men to leave farming and work on huge building projects. Khufu's Great Pyramid is probably the largest free-standing single building ever constructed. Its base covers an area equal to six football pitches and is a true square to within two cm. Some of the building stone was cut from distant quarries and floated down the Nile by raft.

Handmade bricks

Smaller pyramids were often made of mud bricks. These were shaped cheaply and quickly in simple wooden moulds and then left to harden in the sun. Mud bricks were also used to build houses.

Egyptian engineers had only the muscle power of men to help them create buildings. Modern engineering projects use wind, water, steam and electricity power.

Inside, pyramid traps were often built to stop robbers reaching the tomb chamber where the body lay.

Great Pyramid of Giza

This pyramid was made of 2.3 million stone blocks weighing over two tonnes. It took 100,000 men 20 years to build.

Stone blocks were dragged up ramps of earth on rollers. Afterwards the ramps were torn down.

Goldsmiths and bricklayers

Egyptian wall paintings show a wide range of craftsmen, from metalworkers and potters to carvers of ivory. Pyramids were often filled with goods like chariots and fine furniture for use in the afterlife.

BUILDERS & BUILDINGS

ANCIENT EGYPT 3000–30 BC

Gift of the Nile

The Greek historian Herodotus called Egypt 'the gift of the Nile'. Every year, as the mountain snow melted in the south, the world's longest river flooded, leaving a thick layer of mud on both sides of its banks. This made it possible to produce at least two, and often three, crops a year. The main crops were wheat for bread and barley for beer. Flax and cotton were grown to make clothing. The people ate a lot of beans, figs, dates, garlic and salad vegetables.

Raising water
This cheap and simple device called a shaduf used a counterweight of stone or mud to lever up water from one level to the next. It is still in use today.

The Nile Delta
For most of its length the banks of the Nile were fertile for only a few kilometres either side before desert took over. But as the river neared the sea, it fanned out to make a delta 240 km wide. This rich, marshy region was rich in fish and wildfowl to vary the local diet. Marshy areas yielded reeds which were woven to make baskets, ropes, sleeping mats, shoes and even boats.

Irrigation
Egyptian farmers became expert in digging and controlling complex systems of canals, basins, dams and tanks to distribute and store the water of the great river so that it could be used to best effect.

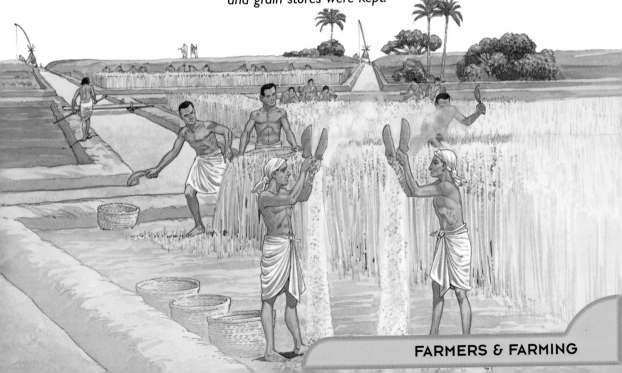

Rich harvest

All land was, in theory, owned by the pharaoh. The pharaoh looked after his people by setting aside some of each year's grain crop in huge stores, to control distribution. If the harvest failed, this grain could be used to make up the shortfall and prevent famine.

Egypt's lifeline

The Nile held Egypt together. Without the cheap method of transport it provided it would not have been possible for Thebes and Luxor to grow into great cities by relying on food transported over long distances. Reeds growing along the river's banks yielded papyrus on which records of taxes and grain stores were kept.

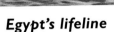

FARMERS & FARMING

Early writing systems

Ancient Iraq and Egypt developed writing systems to record information about taxes, land grants, religious beliefs and histories. With writing they could also send letters to other rulers, record treaties and make inscriptions on buildings and in public places. Iraq's writing-system, known as cuneiform, was based on wedge-shaped marks in clay tablets. In Egypt, where a kind of paper was made from papyrus, writing was done with reed pens, using black and red inks.

Writing in pictures
Egyptian hieroglyphs stood for objects or sounds. About 700 were in common use but there were over 6000 in all. Hieroglyphs could be written from right to left, left to right and up and down.

Schooling for boys
Scribes usually took their own sons as pupils. It took years to master hieroglyphs so fewer than one in 200 Egyptians were fully literate.

The Rosetta Stone

Discovered in Egypt in 1799, the Rosetta Stone carried an inscription which said the same thing in hieroglyphs (top), in a simplified hieroglyphic script called demotic (middle) and in ancient Greek (bottom).

Making paper

Paper was made by sticking together layers of strips made from the pith of the papyrus reed. Papyrus lasted, so it was good for keeping records on. It became one of Egypt's main exports.

Breaking codes

Before the discovery of the Rosetta Stone (above), the secret of reading hieroglyphs had been lost. The french Jean-Francois Champollion and the english Thomas Young puzzled out the answer between them by comparing the Greek text on the stone (which they could read) with the two Egyptian texts.

Tending the dead

Egyptians preserved the bodies of their dead. It was essential that the body did not decay so that body and spirit could be reunited in the afterlife. At first they buried bodies in the desert sand, where they dried out. But jackals often dug up the bodies to eat. So they began putting them in wooden boxes or wicker baskets. But this separated the body from the hot, dry sand which killed off bacteria and bodies buried like this rotted. After centuries of trial and error an effective method of preserving bodies was developed.

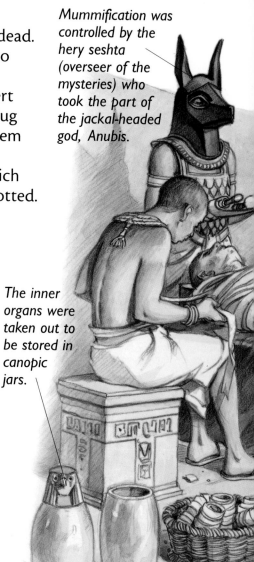

Mummification was controlled by the hery seshta (overseer of the mysteries) who took the part of the jackal-headed god, Anubis.

The inner organs were taken out to be stored in canopic jars.

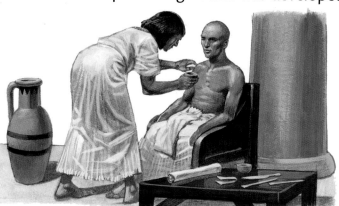

National health

The government paid doctors to give free treatment to travellers and soldiers at war. Egyptian doctors specialized in treating different parts of the body. The pharaoh had a different doctor for each eye!

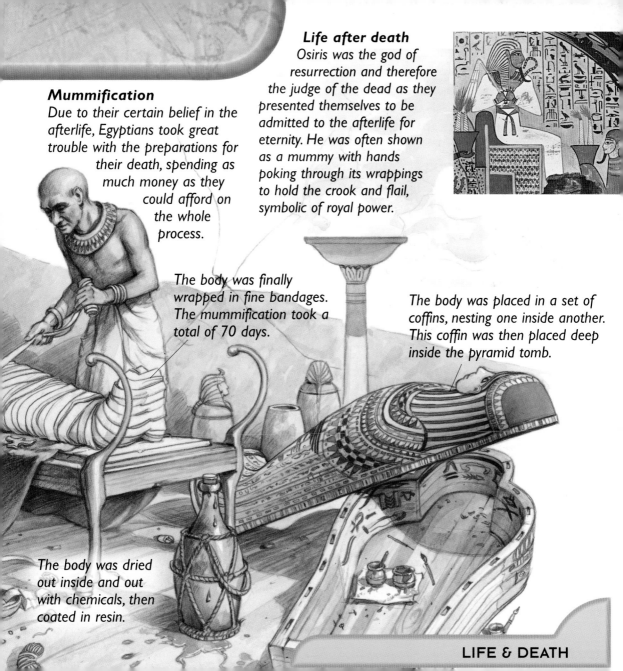

Mummification

Due to their certain belief in the afterlife, Egyptians took great trouble with the preparations for their death, spending as much money as they could afford on the whole process.

Life after death

Osiris was the god of resurrection and therefore the judge of the dead as they presented themselves to be admitted to the afterlife for eternity. He was often shown as a mummy with hands poking through its wrappings to hold the crook and flail, symbolic of royal power.

The body was finally wrapped in fine bandages. The mummification took a total of 70 days.

The body was placed in a set of coffins, nesting one inside another. This coffin was then placed deep inside the pyramid tomb.

The body was dried out inside and out with chemicals, then coated in resin.

LIFE & DEATH

For gods and heroes

Much Greek art was intended to honour gods or great leaders through sculpture or painting. Battles, real or legendary, were a favourite subject. Statues were made for temples and public squares. Paintings done on wood, leather, textiles and the walls of rooms have almost all perished. Only paintings on vases have survived in any quantity because the paint was baked into the clay. Although a few of the greatest artists were respected, most were regarded as no better than common craftsmen because they worked with their hands like a potter or a shoemaker.

Carpet of stones

Mosaic pavements became increasingly common in wealthy Greek houses from the 4th century BC onwards. Under the Romans they were mass-produced for use in public buildings such as baths.

Ideal form

These columns of the Temple of Nike, goddess of victory, on the Acropolis in Athens, show the Greek taste for balance, symmetry and proportion – the style that Europeans came to think of as Classical.

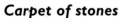

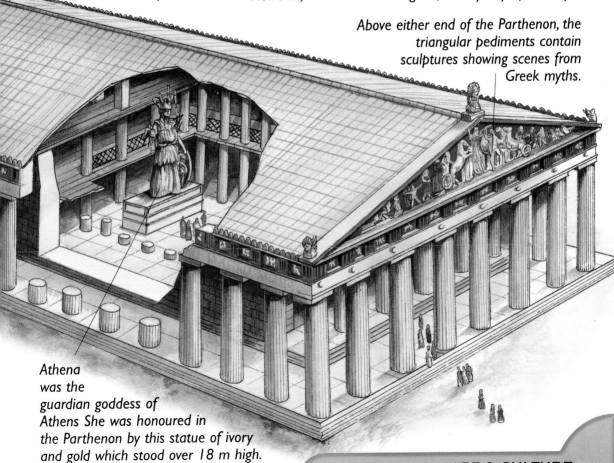

The Parthenon

On a hilltop above Athens stood the Parthenon, a white marble temple. Temples did have priests but worship could also be led by the head of a family. The Greeks, like other peoples, had festivals when whole community worshipped together in the temple. However, Greeks had no regular, weekly day of worship.

Wise owl

Early Greek coins usually carried a symbol of the city which minted them. The owl of wisdom was the emblem of Athena.

Above either end of the Parthenon, the triangular pediments contain sculptures showing scenes from Greek myths.

Athena was the guardian goddess of Athens She was honoured in the Parthenon by this statue of ivory and gold which stood over 18 m high.

The birth of medicine

Doctors in ancient Greece understood the importance of diet, rest, massage and exercise. They knew how to use drugs to relieve pain, to give sleep and to make people vomit. They could set broken bones and bleed out poisons. They also knew that surgery was usually a risky last resort – patients who did not die of shock and loss of blood often died from infection afterwards. Separate systems of medicine developed in ancient China and India but shared the same general view of the importance of diet, the use of drugs and the dangers of surgery. Doctors in all three systems also believed in astrology – that the movements of the stars and planets could tell when the best time was to use a particular form of treatment.

The Hippocratic Oath

Hippocrates, a Greek doctor of the 4th century BC, drew up an oath binding doctors only to use their skill to heal patients and never to harm them. As a doctor, Hippocrates taught the importance of fresh air, cleanliness and a balanced diet. He also knew it was important to keep a record of each individual's illness and how it developed.

Lessons in medicine

All educated men had some knowledge of medicine which they learnt alongside other subjects, including sport. Specialist doctors trained at medical schools like the one on the island of Kos, where Hippocrates taught.

The four humours

Greek medical theory believed that good health depended on a proper balance between the four body fluids — blood, phlegm, yellow bile and black bile. If there was too much or too little of one, the patient would suffer in body or mind until the balance had been corrected by treatment such as sweating, bleeding or vomiting. This idea remained the backbone of medical thinking in Europe until the great scientific advances of the 16th and 17th centuries.

The healing god

Asclepius was the Greek and Roman god of healing. His sign, a staff and serpent, is still often used as the badge of medical organizations.

The gladiators' doctor

Greek medical knowledge was summed up by Galen who lived in the 2nd century AD. He went to Rome and became personal doctor to three Roman emperors. Galen was the first to use the pulse as a way of finding out about a patient's condition. His teachings helped others to learn for more than a thousand years after his death. Galen's theories were based on what he learnt from his early experience as surgeon to gladiators.

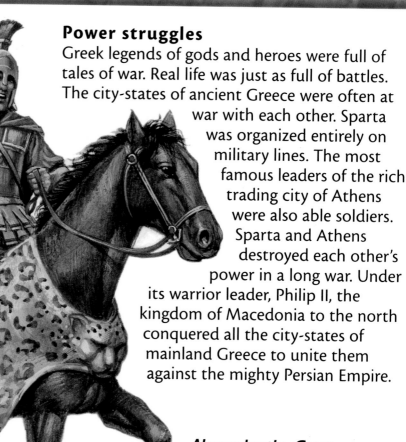

Power struggles

Greek legends of gods and heroes were full of tales of war. Real life was just as full of battles. The city-states of ancient Greece were often at war with each other. Sparta was organized entirely on military lines. The most famous leaders of the rich trading city of Athens were also able soldiers. Sparta and Athens destroyed each other's power in a long war. Under its warrior leader, Philip II, the kingdom of Macedonia to the north conquered all the city-states of mainland Greece to unite them against the mighty Persian Empire.

Alexander the Great

Son of Philip II, Alexander (356–323 BC) carried out his father's plan to conquer Persia and led his armies as far as India before turning back. He founded the port of Alexandria in Egypt and many other cities but his empire fell apart after his early death.

Great thinkers

The Greeks were intensely curious about the world around them. The great teacher Socrates (469–399 BC, left) wrote nothing, but his method of learning through questioning was recorded by his pupil Plato (428–347 BC). Plato's main interest was politics. His pupil, Aristotle (384–322 BC, right) was interested in everything, from politics to plants and even planets. Aristotle was, in turn, Alexander the Great's tutor.

Alexander's coins

Although Alexander's empire died with him his excellent coinage lived on – a lasting symbol of power. From Macedonia to Babylon his mints had turned out a vast quantity of coins of uniform types and weights. They spread the idea that coins should carry a ruler's name. Soon coins carried their portrait as well.

Wall of spears

Greeks fought as compact bodies (phalanxes) of heavily-armed infantry in ranks up to eight deep. Their main weapon was a long spear. It was almost impossible to give changes of orders in the din of battle. The skill of a great leader like Alexander the Great was in choosing the lie of the land to give his army the best advantage before fighting actually began.

The competitors
Only men were allowed to compete in the Olympic Games. Women were not even allowed to be present as spectators. There were separate games for women, although these only involved running races.

Playing to win
Many Greek athletes were professionals, specializing in a single event. As there were many lesser events, apart from the Olympics, they could make a living by travelling from one to another.

Judges and rules
Cheating was severely punished by the judges. In ancient Greece only slaves could normally be beaten as a punishment. But cheats at the Games could also be made to pay for sacrifices to the gods.

Perfect bodies
Ancient Greeks thought the athlete was a symbol of human perfection.

The Olympic Games

Ancient Greece consisted of some 300 city-states which were often at war with each other. Sporting competitions grew out of the sort of training young men undertook to make them fit for all the fighting they had to do – running, wrestling, chariot-racing and throwing the javelin. The first Olympic Games were held in 776 BC. The Greeks divided time itself into the four-year periods which separated each Olympiad from the last. During the Games there was a truce in all wars so that contestants and spectators could travel to the Games. The Greeks saw the Games as an exhibition of courage, fitness and the beauty of the human body.

Prizes for the winners
Sporting heroes were rewarded with jars of olive oil or laurel wreaths as prizes. The real prize was fame and the glory it brought to a winner's home city. Sporting heroes were often honoured by their fellow citizens with statues, pensions and free meals for life.

A trip to the theatre
Greek drama included both tragedies and comedies. Actors wore masks and were often accompanied by a chorus and music. Greek open-air theatres provided entertainment for up to 12,000 people. They had superb acoustics so that even people sitting right at the back could hear clearly.

TIME OFF

THE ROMAN EMPIRE 27 BC–AD 476

Debating skills

The senators discussed laws and government plans in the courtroom. Ambitious young Romans learnt rhetoric, the art of persuasive public speaking. Many of their teachers were Greeks.

The Senate

When Rome was a republic (before 31 BC), the Senate was the most powerful part of the government and it remained an important advisory body when it was ruled by emperors. Augustus set membership at 600. Senators were mostly large landowners. The most influential came from ancient, noble families. As the power of emperors increased, the Senate's direct powers of government became limited to Rome itself. Rule by emperors led to civil wars as ambitious generals used their soldiers to seize the imperial throne by force.

Power

Even though the power of the Senate declined under the Empire, its magnificent buildings and solemn debates made it seem as if it still mattered.

The accused

He could be forced to attend court if necessary.

A helping hand

As large landowners and heads of families, senators were expected to look after the interests of their tenants in law cases and find jobs in the army or government service for their relatives.

Emperors and empire

The Roman republic fell in a power struggle between Julius Caesar and his enemies. They murdered Caesar in 43 BC but were then defeated by his adopted son and heir, who became Rome's first emperor, Augustus, in 27 BC. The empire reached its peak under the first non-Roman to become emperor, Trajan, a Spanish soldier. In 395, Diocletian split the empire into two halves. The eastern half became the powerful empire of Byzantium, bordered by another powerful empire, Persia.

Room to view
Interested citizens could watch from the viewing gallery.

Senate factions
Senators gathered in this hall before entering a courtroom.

Face of power
Romans knew which government they were living under from what appeared on the coinage. Under the republic, coins bore pictures of Roman gods, under the empire, portraits of emperors.

Great thinkers

The Romans were less interested than the Greeks in abstract ideas. The best Roman thinkers excelled in history and the law. Cicero (106–43 BC) studied rhetoric for three years in Greece and became a brilliantly successful lawyer, writer and politician – until he was executed!

Augustus Caesar
Augustus was a brilliant organizer. He rebuilt Rome and gave it water supplies, a fire brigade and police force. Augustus also reformed the Senate and army, and founded a navy. The system of government he created lasted for two centuries after his death.

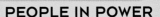

PEOPLE IN POWER

High-rise homes

The Romans invented apartment blocks called insulae, although unlike housing blocks of today, theirs only ran to three or four storeys. They were mostly for poor people who made up the bulk of Rome's population of over a million. The blocks were well serviced, but fire was a constant danger in the overcrowded insulae, as people often cooked meals in their rooms. Many blocks had a cookshop at the ground-floor level, selling fast food.

Hygiene for health

The Romans understood the need for hygiene and proper sanitation in crowded cities to prevent disease. Public toilets were built over channels of running water to flush away the waste.

Home entertainment
The wealthy gave banquets for friends. Nine was considered the ideal number for a dinner party. Guests ate lying on their sides on couches. Entertainment was provided by professional dancers, singers, jugglers, acrobats or conjurers.

Luxurious living
While poor city-dwellers lived in crowded apartments the rich lived in extravagant villas. Poor people went to the public baths and drew water from public fountains. Rich ones had their own bathroom suites, piped water and underfloor heating. High walls, string gates and small outer windows gave villas security and concealed the wealth within. Fine Roman roads enabled the rich to travel to second homes at the seaside or in the country.

Carried away
Wealthy women and old or sick people travelled in curtained litters carried by a team of slaves.

Inventive engineering

The Romans used the styles of architecture developed by the Greeks, whose temples they greatly admired. Many great engineering projects were the work of the Roman army. In Britain, Roman soldiers built Hadrian's Wall which runs 117 km, from one side of the country to the other. Enormous public bath-houses with complicated plumbing and heating systems were a major feature of every sizeable Roman town. The actual running of baths, amphitheatres, aqueducts and other public facilities usually relied on the labour of slaves.

Deadly entertainment

The Colosseum in Rome was completed in AD 80. It was a huge building, devoted to the entertainment of the masses. Sitting on three levels, 50,000 spectators could watch gladiators fight each other and wild animals kill Christians. It could be flooded to stage mock sea-battles and covered with an awning in hot weather to shade the crowd.

Water transportation

With a million inhabitants, Rome needed huge volumes of water for drinking, cooking, washing, bathing, and industry. By AD 97 nine aqueducts brought in 320 million litres of water a day from mountain springs. Two hundred other Roman cities also had aqueducts.

Roman road-building

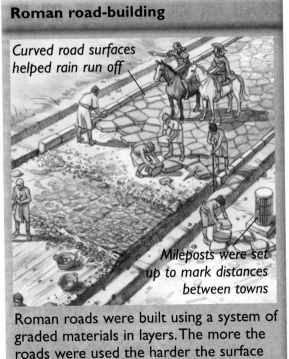

Curved road surfaces helped rain run off

Mileposts were set up to mark distances between towns

Roman roads were built using a system of graded materials in layers. The more the roads were used the harder the surface became as the weight of the traffic compressed the layers together.

The gladiators' doctor

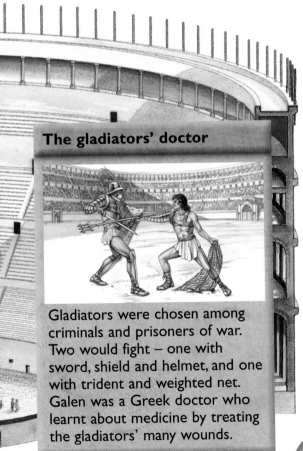

Gladiators were chosen among criminals and prisoners of war. Two would fight – one with sword, shield and helmet, and one with trident and weighted net. Galen was a Greek doctor who learnt about medicine by treating the gladiators' many wounds.

THE ROMAN EMPIRE 27 BC–AD 476

Organized manpower

The Roman army originally consisted of native-born Roman citizens but as the empire expanded it took in men from conquered territories. The army was divided into legions of roughly 6000 men, which had the full range of skills to fight as independent units. Roman troops were extremely well-drilled and trained and frequently beat armies far larger in number through sheer discipline and method. The Roman army was extremely well-organized, like most areas of life in the Roman Empire.

Battle gear

Roman soldiers in close combat used a short, heavy stabbing sword, protecting themselves with a long, curved shield, flexible body armour and close-fitting helmet contoured to ward off blows to the face and neck.

Camp building

A Roman legion included trained masons, carpenters and surveyors. Here they are shown constructing a powerful stone fortress as a defensive base. They could also put up camps of wood and earth in a few hours.

The Roman soldier

The core of the army consisted of long-service professional soldiers trained to fight as heavily-armed infantry. Roman soldiers on the march cooked for themselves in mess-groups of ten, sharing the same tent. Each legionary was expected to carry 132 kg of weapons, supplies and equipment.

Cavalry officer

Legionary
A soldier carried all his equipment and supplies with him on a march.

Protective shell
Legionaries facing a barrage of stones or a shower of spears and arrows would form a testudo (tortoise) to protect themselves while advancing to close combat.

Precious books

In medieval Europe books were written on vellum, a very fine kind of parchment made from the skin of a calf, kid or lamb. Preparing a single sheet of vellum took many hours of careful scraping and softening. To make a copy of the New Testament of the Bible used three hundred lambs' skins. As it might also take three years for a scribe to copy out the text this meant that books were incredibly precious. A monastery with fifty books would have had a large library. Monasteries loaned books to each other so that they could be copied.

Illumination
Books were illuminated with brilliantly coloured initial letters and drawings in the margin. These were not just for decoration but acted as markers to help the reader find particular passages of text faster.

Team effort
Making a book needed the skills of many craftsmen — to prepare vellum, ink and pens, to write the text and paint illuminations and to make a cover of wood and leather.

Tales of gods

Vikings had little use for books and writing but loved tales of battles and monsters. So Viking bards memorized long poems, called sagas, about their gods and heroes.

Book of Kells

This ornamented gospel was probably begun on the Scottish island of Iona in the 8th century. After Viking raids began in 795 the book was taken to Kells in Ireland to be completed safely.

Devastation by fire

Throughout the Middle Ages, war, not peace, was the normal state of affairs throughout Europe. After the break-up of the Roman Empire, in the fifth century, Christian Europe was tormented by raids and invasions by Muslims from the south, Vikings from the north and pagan Balts, Letts and Magyars from the east. In later centuries strong kingdoms made war on each other to enlarge their territories. The most widely-used weapon was fire – immensely destructive to homes and barns made of wood, and fields full of grain. The Church tried to limit the damage by teaching that priests and other innocent people should be spared from harm.

Mantlet

Crossbowman

Longboat explorers

Viking raiders from Scandinavia were great seafarers who sailed around Western Europe in open longboats, pillaging for treasure and slaves. Later, Vikings settled in England, Normandy and the Scottish Islands.

Under siege

Sieges rather than battles were the most common form of medieval warfare. Castles were rarely taken by storm and could usually hold out providing they had enough food and water. Besieging armies were often destroyed by disease and desertion. Here mangonels batter rocks against castle walls while wooden assault towers, built for use during a seige, are wheeled up against them.

Siege-tower

Scaling ladder

Mangonel

Killer epidemics

An epidemic is an outbreak of disease bad enough to wipe out a whole community. Ancient Greece, Rome and Byzantium all suffered epidemics which killed millions, and terrified survivors by their scale and suddenness. Infections spread quickly among people living close together in crowded, dirty conditions, with poor sanitation. Safety lay in flight from the infection. Epidemics led to deserted cities and abandoned fields and were therefore often followed by famines. It could take decades or even centuries for populations to recover to former levels.

Bubonic plague
Bites from the fleas carried in rats' fur spread the bubonic plague. An even more deadly form, pneumonic plague, could be caught by breathing in droplets from the breath of an infected person.

Disappearing children

The Pied Piper was said to have charmed away rats from Hamelin in Germany. Refused payment, he also charmed away the town's children. The legend may record an epidemic of child deaths.

Leprosy warning

There were epidemics of leprosy in Europe in the 1100s and 1200s. Leprosy, a contagious skin disease, was not usually fatal like the plague, but its unfortunate sufferers often carried clappers like this to warn others to stay away.

'Bring out your dead!'

When plague broke out, a red cross was painted on the door of the sufferer to warn passersby. At night a cart trundled through the streets to carry away the dead bodies.

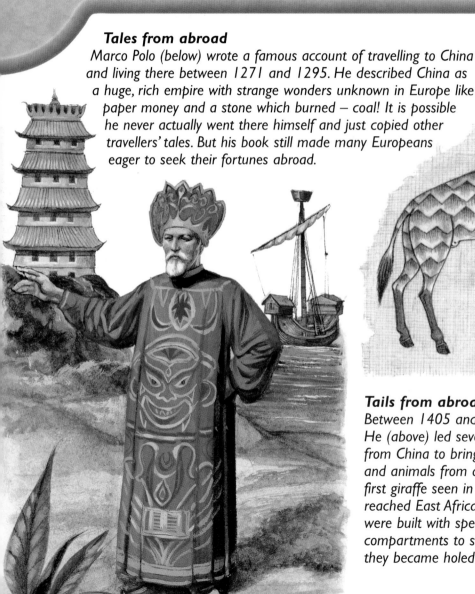

Tales from abroad

Marco Polo (below) wrote a famous account of travelling to China and living there between 1271 and 1295. He described China as a huge, rich empire with strange wonders unknown in Europe like paper money and a stone which burned – coal! It is possible he never actually went there himself and just copied other travellers' tales. But his book still made many Europeans eager to seek their fortunes abroad.

Tails from abroad

Between 1405 and 1433 Admiral Zheng He (above) led seven fleets of junks from China to bring back gifts, goods and animals from abroad, including the first giraffe seen in China. His last voyage reached East Africa. Zheng He's junks were built with special watertight compartments to stop them sinking if they became holed in one place.

Cloves

Precious cargoes

Long-distance trade and travel between Europe and Asia revived only slowly after the break-up of the Roman Empire in the 5th century AD. The high costs and risks of travel at this time limited long-distance trade to very valuable goods such as gemstones, gold, silk, porcelain and carpets. Muslim merchants in the Middle East came to link Europe, Asia and Africa. Muslims shared a common language, Arabic, and common laws which made trading easier for them. New technologies spread along trade routes. Paper-making was invented in China in the 2nd century BC. The secret took a thousand years to reach the Arab world and

Cinnamon another six centuries to get to northern Europe.

Keeping count

Around the 5th century, merchants were usually the only people controlling distribution of goods. They were also the only ones who could read and write, apart from priests, with Chinese and Arabic used as the main trading languages by everyone.

Importing ideas

Until about 1700, Europeans did not know how to make porcelain so they imported it from China and Japan. As well as being beautiful, porcelain is light and heat-proof. Porcelain bowls like this became even more popular when Europeans began to drink tea.

Trade goods

Spices for food, dyes for cloth and drugs for medicine were the most common goods traded over long distances. The most popular spices were pepper, cloves, nutmeg and cinnamon. Most spices came from southern India and Indonesia.

Farming to live

At this time, in Europe, villagers produced most of their own food. In addition, they needed to grow extra crops or fatten animals for sale at the local market. The profit they made could buy iron or salt, things they couldn't make at home.

Thatching
Straw gathered from the fields could be used to thatch roofs.

Serfdom
Most farmers were serfs who paid rent on their land by working two or three days a week for the lord who owned their village.

Non-intensive farming
At this time, labour was carried out using only the power of humans and animals. This did not allow the farmer to farm the land intensively.

Recycling
Pigs and poultry were very useful to villagers because they could survive on kitchen scraps and waste.

Haymaking
This 15th-century illustration shows men and women cutting meadow grass to make hay in June. Hay was stored to feed cattle through the winter.

Sheepshearing
Sheep gave wool to be made into cloth and meat to be eaten. Their milk could be made into cheese, their bones boiled for glue and their horns made into spoons.

FARMERS & FARMING

Religious relics

Relics of saints, in the form of personal belongings or pieces of their bones, were often kept by the faithful. Shown below is a relic in the shape of the Christian symbol of the cross.

Pilgrimages in Europe

A pilgrimage is a journey to a holy place. Christians went on pilgrimage to holy places to ask God for forgiveness from sins, to beg to be healed from an illness or to have a child, or even to give thanks for good fortune. Pilgrimage was the nearest thing there was to going away on holiday. Although it had a serious purpose it also meant seeing new places, meeting new people and buying souvenirs. Some famous pilgrimage places were Jerusalem, Rome and Santiago de Compostela in Spain.

Telling tales

The most famous place of pilgrimage in England was Canterbury Cathedral, where the body of St Thomas à Becket was buried. The poet Geoffrey Chaucer (died 1400) wrote The Canterbury Tales, *a series of stories in verse which were supposed to have been told by a party of pilgrims to pass the time on their long journey from London to Canterbury Cathedral.*

Pilgrimages in Asia

Pilgrimage is also part of the Muslim, Hindu and Buddhist religions. A famous Buddhist pilgrimage route on the Japanese island of Shikoku involved visiting 88 shrines. Another Buddhist pilgrimage was to Kandy in Sri Lanka where it was said there was one of the Buddha's teeth preserved as a relic. Hindus gathered in huge numbers each year at Varanasi to bathe in the waters of the sacred River Ganges. Each year Muslims went on a pilgrimage to Mecca in Arabia, the birthplace of the prophet Muhammad. Afterwards they often visited Medina, where he is buried. Meeting other pilgrims from many different places was an efficient way of spreading news to tell when they returned home.

Safety in numbers
Pilgrims often travelled in groups, partly for company and partly for protection against bandits. The picture above shows Muslim pilgrims leaving Egypt for Mecca. They are being given a noisy send-off by a military band.

Light of faith

The brightly coloured stained-glass windows of medieval cathedrals created a dazzling light show as the sun shifted round the building in the course of a day. Priests used the Bible stories they showed to teach worshippers who could not read or write.

Community effort

Building a castle or palace showed the power of a ruler. Building a cathedral showed the wealth of a community. Most took centuries to complete.

An apprentice learns the skills of his trade.

Glass was made as it was needed.

Strips of lead are joined to hold the glass in place.

A glazier cuts glass to the shape required to fit the window.

Finally, the glazed panels are placed in the stone frame.

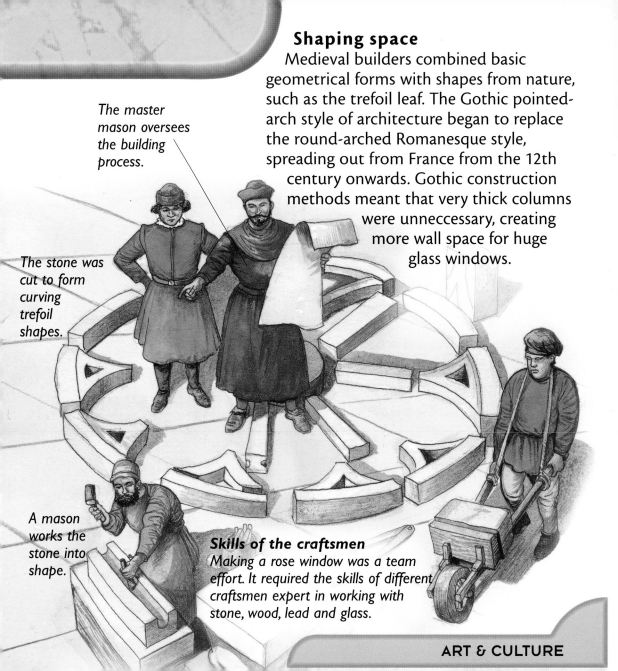

Shaping space

Medieval builders combined basic geometrical forms with shapes from nature, such as the trefoil leaf. The Gothic pointed-arch style of architecture began to replace the round-arched Romanesque style, spreading out from France from the 12th century onwards. Gothic construction methods meant that very thick columns were unneccessary, creating more wall space for huge glass windows.

The master mason oversees the building process.

The stone was cut to form curving trefoil shapes.

A mason works the stone into shape.

Skills of the craftsmen
Making a rose window was a team effort. It required the skills of different craftsmen expert in working with stone, wood, lead and glass.

Home discomforts

Most medieval homes were built on a framework of wooden timbers, with walls of mud smeared over panels of woven sticks. Roofs were made of thick thatch, an ideal home for birds, rats and insects. Floors were made of trodden earth. Windows were covered with oiled parchment which let light through. Smoke from an open fire escaped as best it could. Furniture consisted of rough wooden benches, stools and trestle-tables. Possessions were stored in chests or on pegs and shelves. Dirt and damp were normal and just got worse in winter.

Music for the home

When bad weather kept people indoors they amused themselves with telling tales and asking riddles. Rich people listened to professional minstrels who sang, played and recited stories in verse.

Living with livestock

Chickens and pigs were kept near the house, to be fed on kitchen waste. In winter oxen and cows were often brought inside to stop them from freezing or being stolen. Their body heat helped to keep the house warm.

Letting the light in

The old open fire-pit was replaced by a fireplace and chimney to carry away smoke. Glass windows let in light but kept out rain and draughts.

The comfort revolution

During the 1500s the homes of the better off were rebuilt in stone or brick and became much more comfortable, with a staircase rather than ladders to reach the upper level, tiled or wooden floors and wooden ceilings rather than an open roofspace.

Multi-purpose moat

Large country homes often had a moat, partly for protection against robbers but also to supply water for the home and as somewhere to breed fish.

Country pursuits

Plays and operas could normally only be seen in the palaces of kings or in big cities. However, when theatres were closed on account of the plague, companies of actors took their plays out to the countryside. Most people lived in small towns or villages and shared the same outdoor pleasures. The rich had the leisure to hunt or dance any day they liked. But most people worked long hours and only had time off on holy days or traditional festivals such as May Day, which marked the coming of summer.

War practice
Hunting put food on the table and was also good practice for war. Hunters kept fit and learnt how to ride well and to use bows and spears skilfully.

The Globe Theatre
In Shakespeare's day London's theatres were outside the city walls. The Globe could cram in 3000 people, most of them standing. The growth of professional theatre marked the beginning of entertainment as business.

Holiday fun
Special fairs were held on holidays. Dancing round the maypole was usual on May Day. Baiting bears and bulls with dogs was a popular entertainment.

Favourite sports
Although bows and arrows were no longer used in war, archery remained a popular sport. So did wrestling and fighting with cudgels and quarter-staffs.

TIME OFF

The cult of Elizabeth
Elizabeth I developed the image of a strong, glittering, virgin queen that she stamped on the minds of her people and on her property, including her coins.

Widespread monarchy

The normal form of government in this period, from Europe to China, was monarchy. The republican city-states of Italy and cantons of Switzerland were unusual exceptions. Most rulers increased their power at the expense of elected parliaments or assemblies of nobles. England was rather different. There, conflicts between rulers and parliaments came to show that the country was stronger when they worked together and the monarch's power was eroded.

Monarchy or Republic?
Charles I (1625–1649) tried to rule England without the support of the Parliament. This plunged the country into civil war. Charles lost and was executed in 1649. England became the Commonwealth, a republic. This collapsed with the death of its leader, Oliver Cromwell. In 1660 Charles I's son was restored to the throne as Charles II.

Spymaster-general
Every ruler feared plots against them. Elizabeth I's trusted minister, Francis Walsingham, created Europe's first modern spy service. His well-educated agents worked to uncover traitors of the queen.

The ruler and the people

Ordinary people had little contact with their rulers. Monarchs treated their subjects as an audience to be impressed by their splendid clothes and large armed escorts. Elizabeth had 3000 items of clothing in her wardrobe. When Charles I was executed, he wore two shirts in case he shivered and onlookers might think him a coward.

Emperor Akbar

Akbar means 'great'. He doubled the size of the Mughal Empire in India in a reign of almost fifty years (1556–1605). He was known to be strong enough to kill a tiger with one sword stroke. Akbar also had his artists make him a huge library of illustrated books – even though he never learnt to read.

Elizabeth I

Strong-willed and hardworking, Elizabeth spoke six languages and was an excellent judge of men. Her loyal servants ranged from clever ministers and elegant courtiers to brilliant poets and tough pirates. The defeat of the great Spanish Armada by her navy in 1588 made the English feel that 'Good Queen Bess' had God's special protection.

Protection from pirates

Pirates flourished where they could hide away on small offshore islands and come out to prey on isolated merchant ships. The South China Seas and the Caribbean were ideal for pirates. Merchant ships started to sail heavily armed for protection and often in convoys. Pirates finally lost their grip on the seas with the arrival of fast steamboats, which could hunt the pirates down or just outrun them.

Bandits

Travellers usually went in groups to protect themselves from robbers. When bandits were caught they were often hanged at the scene of their crime as a warning to others.

Stagecoach travel

A return to Roman methods of road-making, using graded layers of stones, made it possible to run regular inter-city horse-drawn coach services. By 1830, British stagecoaches were averaging 13 km/h, carrying mail and passengers.

Reluctant road menders

Local people were often forced to mend the roads passing through their area and so did the job badly. After all, it was strangers who would benefit most.

Carts for the market
Broad-wheeled carts could carry heavy loads to local markets but only went at about 5 km/h.

The dangers of road travel
Roads before 1800 were poorly-made and kept compared with Roman times. Travel was often uncomfortable, tiring and dangerous even in good weather, and sometimes quite impossible in winter. Carriages were only for the very wealthy, women, the old and the sick. Most people walked. Apart from trade the main reason for travelling was pilgrimage to holy places. But kings and rich people travelled to live and hunt on their different estates.

Postman on horse
Governments used messengers on horseback to speed the spread of news by delivering dispatches about major events.

Pedlars
Pedlars walked from village to village selling small things like needles and ribbons. They also helped the spread of news by gossiping about the outside world, often unreliably.

TRAVEL & TRADE

The Sun King
Louis XIV liked to see himself as a brilliant centre around which the world, or at least his court, revolved, as the planets revolved round the Sun. Louis used the Sun as a symbol of his power.

Dazzling palaces

At five, Louis XIV (1638–1715) became king of France, the richest and most powerful country in Europe. In fact Louis declared, 'I am the State', and set about showing off his wealth and glory through extravagance in all things. Royal factories and workshops were founded to produce furniture, clocks and ceramics to decorate the king's palaces. At Versailles, outside Paris, from 1669 onwards Louis began building a royal residence which dazzled all of Europe and was widely copied for a century.

The gardens of Versailles
The gardens around the palace of Versailles were laid out by master designer André Le Nôtre. He transformed a muddy swamp into 6070 hectares of majestic parks, woods and planted beds, full of statues and spectacular waterworks.

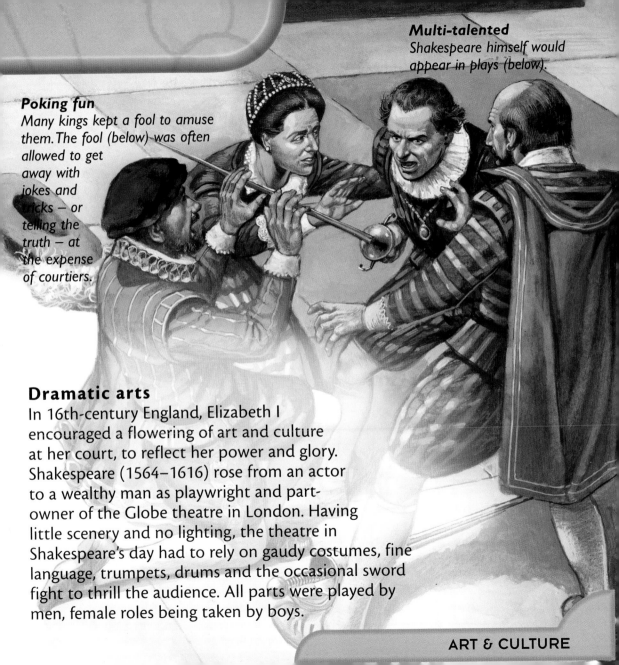

Multi-talented
Shakespeare himself would appear in plays (below).

Poking fun
Many kings kept a fool to amuse them. The fool (below) was often allowed to get away with jokes and tricks — or telling the truth — at the expense of courtiers.

Dramatic arts

In 16th-century England, Elizabeth I encouraged a flowering of art and culture at her court, to reflect her power and glory. Shakespeare (1564–1616) rose from an actor to a wealthy man as playwright and part-owner of the Globe theatre in London. Having little scenery and no lighting, the theatre in Shakespeare's day had to rely on gaudy costumes, fine language, trumpets, drums and the occasional sword fight to thrill the audience. All parts were played by men, female roles being taken by boys.

Sail power

By 1400 ships used sails of different sizes and shapes so that they could move forward even when the wind was not blowing directly that way. By 1500 Portuguese sailors had reached Brazil and found a sea-route to India by sailing right round Africa. But storms and calms, changing winds and tides meant it was still impossible to say just how many days or months any journey would take.

Navigation

The sailor's biggest problem was simply knowing his ship's location. This depended on having accurate instruments for making observations, measurements and calculations based on landmarks, winds, tides and the Sun, Moon and stars.

Recording information
Before the invention of photography, artists were taken on voyages. Cook's artist, Parkinson (below), is drawing the plant Banksia (named after Joseph Banks).

Telescope

Compass

Steam train

The earliest locomotives were built to haul coal from mines to waterways. In 1830 a new line was opened to carry both goods and passengers between the city of Manchester and the port of Liverpool.

Captain Cook's adventures

Captain James Cook (1728–1779) of the Royal Navy mapped more of the world than any other single person. His exploration ships were originally built for the British coastal coal trade but carried him on three great voyages round the world. Cook proved that New Zealand was two islands and not part of Australia. He was also the first seafarer to sail into Antarctic waters and prove that there was no great undiscovered 'Southern Continent'. Cook's voyages brought back a wealth of information about new territories.

Botanical Banks

Scientist Joseph Banks (1744–1820) sailed with Cook on his first voyage and brought back 3000 plants – 1400 of them were unknown to Europeans. He founded the Royal Botanic Gardens at Kew, England, to study plants.

TRAVEL & TRADE

Building with wood

In countries with big forests, like Norway or Japan, most buildings and bridges were made of wood rather than stone or brick. Ornamentation of buildings therefore required different skills of joinery, carving or patterning. Fires and damp have destroyed most old wooden structures but some outstanding examples have survived for as long as 1200 years. In Japan craftsmen used great skill in mixing hard and soft woods to make earthquake-proof buildings.

Handmade details

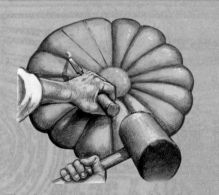

The Japanese emperors' badge is shaped like a chrysanthemum with sixteen petals. It therefore adorns many of the royal palaces.

Nijo Castle

Built in the 17th century in the Japanese city of Kyoto, Nijo Castle was a residence for the shogun (military dictator). This magnificent gateway is built in a Chinese style. The simpler Japanese style can be seen behind it. Nijo Castle is famous for its floors which squeak when people walk on them, warning the guards of intruders.

Stone for the wealthy

The expense of quarrying, transporting and carving stone meant that it was mostly used for important or special buildings such as castles, cathedrals, churches and palaces. Sometimes, less prominent buildings and walls were made cheaply in brick or cemented rubble and covered with an outer layer of stone.

The Taj Mahal
This tomb for the wife of the Mughal emperor, Shah Jahan, was completed around 1650 at Agra in India. The Taj Mahal is built of white marble, inlaid with semi-precious stones. It took 20,000 men 20 years to build.

Fighting with guns

The American Civil War (1861–1865) was one of the bloodiest conflicts of the 19th century. The Southern states were fighting an army from their own country for the right to withdraw from the Union of states that made up America. The Southerners wanted to form a separate Confederate States of America in order to preserve slavery. At the time when the war began, America had few professional soldiers. Fighting between untrained armies led to massive casualties.

Lack of weapons
The Confederate (Southern) army had good leadership, but the industries in its power could not produce enough weapons and equipment for the men.

Loading a musket
The single-shot musket was loaded using a ram-rod to tamp the ball and charge down the barrel. This had to be done standing up, exposing the soldier to enemy fire.

Uniform style
Some American military favoured a Gallic-style uniform. The 5th New York Zouaves, (right) adopted this style — baggy trousers, braided jacket and tassled fez.

Horsepower
Both sides used cavalry for scouting, sudden attacks in battle and to conduct hit-and-run raids.

Industrial strength
Not only could the Union (Northern) army rely on most of America's industry to supply it, but it could also draw on a far larger population for recruits.

Artillery
Field artillery, hauled by horses, could be moved rapidly around the battlefield. Much heavier siege artillery was used to batter forts and cities into surrender.

Missing men
At the first Battle of Bull Run (above) in 1861, 378 Confederate men were recorded dead with 1489 wounded. The Union had 481 dead and 1011 wounded.
However, the Confederates only admitted to 30 men missing whilst the Union recorded 1400 missing – suggesting that the Confederate numbers could have been far from the truth.

Bestseller divides a nation

Uncle Tom's Cabin showed the horrors of slavery in the American South. Published in 1852, it brought thousands of new supporters to the struggle against slavery.

Multiple copies

Printing was first developed in Korea and China around the 8th century and used to make copies of Buddhist religious teachings and prayers. European printers first used carved wooden blocks to make cheap religious pictures to be sold to pilgrims as souvenirs. Printing from reusable metal was perfected in the mid-15th century by Johannes Gutenberg. William Caxton brought printing to England in 1476.

135,000 SETS, 270,000 VOLUMES SOLD.

UNCLE TOM'S CABIN

FOR SALE HERE.

AN EDITION FOR THE MILLION, COMPLETE IN 1 Vol., PRICE 37 1-2 CENTS.
" " IN GERMAN, IN 1 Vol., PRICE 50 CENTS.
" " IN 2 Vols., CLOTH, 6 PLATES, PRICE $1.50.
SUPERB ILLUSTRATED EDITION, IN 1 Vol., WITH 153 ENGRAVINGS,
PRICES FROM $2.50 TO $5.00.

The Greatest Book of the Age.

Printed Bible

The invention of printing made it possible to produce a Bible for a tenth of the price of a handwritten copy and a hundred times as fast. Cheap printed Bibles put religion into the hands of ordinary people and helped spread Protestantism in Europe.

Spreading news

The earliest type of press (right) used a screw mechanism, like a press for squeezing the juice from grapes or olives. It was slow to operate. Later a counterweight was invented, designed to lift the printing-plate automatically after each sheet was printed. This press was three times faster. As a result it became possible to print thousands of daily newspapers quickly. The first daily papers appeared in Germany in the 1660s.

Gutenberg press

Art and advertizing

The Japanese were the first to master multi-coloured printing using carved wooden blocks from around 1740. Coloured prints were used to advertize plays and restaurants or to depict travel scenes for sale as souvenirs. These prints were not thought of as great art at the time, as they are now.

Playing cards

These were one of the earliest printed products. These three depict characters in 17th-century costume but were actually printed in 1820 in Germany.

Coketown

Charles Dickens' Coketown was an imaginary industrial city in one of Britain's manufacturing regions. He described it as permanently shrouded in smoke and smeared with soot from factory chimneys. Coal had created a whole new way of life. It drove the steam engines which powered factories and locomotives. It made the bricks for buildings and provided the gas which lit them. Coal fires heated homes and boiled the water for washing and cooking and bathing. Coal made the iron used for a hundred everyday things, from railways to frying-pans. Coal was essential to keep a home warm and comfortable – but the housewife's life was a constant battle against the filth it created. However, this air pollution, along with foul water supplies and dirty drains meant town dwellers lived with the constant threat of an epidemic.

Home, sweet home?

As more work was done in factories rather than home workshops, the worlds of work and home became more separate. But without buses or bicycles most people had to live within walking distance of the factory. This exposed their homes to pollution.

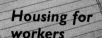

Housing for workers

Riding high

Early bicycles were known as 'boneshakers' and were only for the young and fit. They were also much too expensive for general use.

Smoking chimneys day and night

Cotton mill

The edge of town

Chapel

Factory

Smoke from railway

Coal heap creates dust

Horse droppings fouled roads

72

Goods train

Culture for consumers

As the Industrial Revolution made countries richer, so people began to have more money to spend on themselves – creating a demand for mass-produced art and entertainment. The results included cheaply-produced books, sheet music and cheap musical instruments, as well as ornaments and pictures to decorate the home. Outside the home the entertainment included beer-houses and gin-shops, boxing booths, freak-shows, travelling menageries and down-market music halls offering sing-songs, jugglers and short, silly plays about lovers or murderers.

William Morris

In reaction to cheap, ugly machine-made goods, William Morris (1834–1896) tried to revive the skills of the medieval craftsmen who created beautiful things regardless of profit. Morris's firm made stained-glass and furniture for churches, and wallpaper, curtains and furniture for the home. William Morris was also famous as a poet and an expert on eastern carpets. He campaigned to protect ancient buildings and in his old age revived the art of printing beautiful books.

Art and advertizing

As printing improved, advertizers could employ more skilled artists to create posters and packaging. Bubbles, used to sell Pears Soap, was painted by Sir John Everett Millais, the President of the Royal Academy.

Travelling circus
The first circus was created by Philip Astley in London in 1768. As roads improved, by around 1830 there were a growing number of travelling circuses.

In the ring
A typical circus combined displays of horsemanship with tumblers, jugglers and wild animals such as elephants. Later circuses, after around 1850, featured trapeze acts, clowns and lion-tamers as popular ringside acts.

AGE OF STEAM & IRON 1779–1850

Mechanized farming

By the mid-19th century steam-powered machinery was being used by the wealthier farmers in Europe and America. Industry also supplied cheap iron tools, clay pipes to drain heavy soils and tiles to replace thatch on roofs.

Steam-powered farming

Linked up to the threshing machine, the steam engine could complete the job in a fraction of the time it used to take. Farming was becoming more intensive.

Horsepower

Horses still provided the main driving power on farms. Even the power of new engineering like steam engines was measured in units of horsepower!

Mixed farming

Many farms both produced crops and raised livestock, rather than specializing in either. This was less risky than relying on a single product which could be wiped out by drought or disease.

Machine workers

While farmers prospered their labourers rarely did. Harvest time meant very long hours but in winter there was often little work, so little pay. As labourers left the land for better jobs in factories or to emigrate overseas, farmers brought in machines to do more work with fewer men.

Sheepshearing

Many farmers had huge flocks of sheep. The wool from their fleeces was always in demand.

TAYLOR

FARMERS & FARMING

Efficient techniques

The first iron bridge in the world was built at Ironbridge, Shropshire in 1779. During the Industrial Revolution, mass-produced iron became cheap enough to use for building, but the industry was slow to adopt machinery and new construction methods. Early canals and railways were built using horses and men to shift tonnes of earth and stone. Steam power did aid big projects later, like building bridges, by driving cranes and pile-drivers. Railways meant bricks, slates and timber could be carried long distances cheaply. Steam-powered machinery could be used to mass produce building materials.

Crystal Palace
This building was constructed of standardized iron sections in just four months, even though it was over 600 m long. It was built to house the Great Exhibition of 1851 in London's Hyde Park.

Mass-produced glass

The Crystal Palace needed 294,000 glass panes. Each one was made at exactly the same size, making them much cheaper to produce than if they had been different sizes.

Temporary structures

After the Great Exhibition ended, the Crystal Palace was taken down and rebuilt in southeast London for use as a leisure centre. During the Crimean War of 1854–1856, the British engineer Isambard Kingdom Brunel designed a prefabricated hospital ward which could be put up near a battlefield with mostly unskilled labour. Some architects today are deliberately designing buildings, such as London's Millennium Dome, to have a limited lifespan.

Eiffel Tower
Named after its designer, Gustav Eiffel, it was built in 1889 to commemorate the World's fair held to mark the centenary of the French Revolution. It was meant to last only 20 years.

Chicago skyscrapers
The construction methods pioneered by the Crystal Palace were later used to build the first skyscrapers in Chicago and New York in the 1880s and 1890s.

Fighting infection

By the 18th century it was known that giving people a mild dose of smallpox, by scratching their skin and deliberately infecting them with it, could make them safe from it in later life. This was known as inoculation. The problem was to ensure the dose was a weak one. In 1796 the English doctor, Edward Jenner, discovered that a mild dose of cowpox gave protection with much less risk.

'King Cholera'

Cholera from India reached Britain in 1831 to kill 50,000. Only much later was it understood that it was spread by infected water supplies. The answer was better sanitation.

Saving lives

Edward Jenner was a village doctor in Gloucestershire, England. His discovery made him famous but not rich because he gave away his secret and preferred to live quietly. Jenner's discovery was called 'vaccination' from the Latin for cow (vacca). The use of vaccinations spread quickly, saving millions of lives.

Research for cures

Progress in science began to provide doctors with increasingly effective treatments as throughout the 19th century. French scientist Louis Pasteur developed vaccines to treat deadly diseases like rabies and anthrax. English doctor Joseph Lister used germ-killing antiseptics to more than halve the death rate from infections after surgery. Anaesthetics were used to end the agony of surgery.

Germ killer
Pasteur had the idea that diseases were caused by germs. Lister applied the theory to surgery, using an antiseptic chemical spray to kill germs and so fight infection.

The Curies
In 1903 Marie and Pierre Curie were awarded the Nobel Prize for discovering radium, which can cause – and cure – cancer. Later Marie worked on X-rays. Sadly she died of radiation poisoning. Her notebooks are still too radioactive to be handled safely.

The Hippocratic Oath

Thomas Wakley founded the medical journal The Lancet to set standards and expose frauds who set themselves up as doctors. These fakes went against the principles of the Hippocratic Oath by putting their patients lives at risk through incompetence.

Women in medicine
During the 19th century Florence Nightingale developed a proper training system for nurses. Elizabeth Garret Anderson (above) qualified as Britain's first woman doctor in 1865 after being refused training by three universities. The dispensary she founded in 1866 is now a women's hospital named after her.

LIFE & DEATH

The spread of English

The growth of Britain's trade and powerful empire made English the global language of commerce and learning. During the 19th century English overtook French as the language of international politics. English has the great advantage of being a language that is quite easy to learn – at least enough to be more or less understood. It is now the world's most widely spoken second language and it is the standard language of aviation, science, medicine and computing.

North America

Pacific Ocean

School for success
In 1800s' America immigrants from all nations were eager for their children to learn English at school in order to succeed in life.

Alice in Wonderland
Books printed on steam powered presses became cheap enough to be given to children. Characters like Alice (left) became known and loved across the English-speaking world in the 1800s.

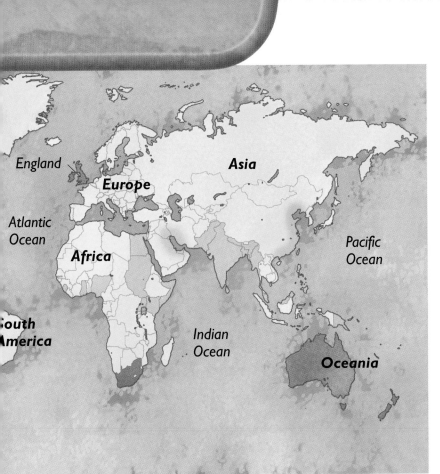

England
Europe
Asia
Atlantic
Ocean
Africa
Pacific
Ocean
South
America
Indian
Ocean
Oceania

Charles Dickens
As a novelist, Dickens (1813–1870) became rich and famous on both sides of the Atlantic. Since his death, his characters have been reborn many times through films, radio and TV.

Key to map

English spoken as a first language

English used as a government language

English spoken among traders

Language of order and business

English became the main spoken language of the British Isles, North America, the Caribbean and Oceania, as shown on the map (above). Through the growth of the British Empire, it became the language of government throughout much of Asia and Africa, and was widely understood by traders in non-English speaking areas like South America, coastal China and the Persian Gulf.

The spread of sport

As the British Empire spread, the British took their sports with them. The army encouraged sports such as boxing, riding and shooting competitions to keep soldiers occupied and fit. In India, army officers developed a local game to invent modern polo. British engineers building railways through remote areas filled in their leisure hours with cricket or soccer. Wherever migrants from Britain founded cities they would usually build a racetrack, and later on, tennis courts. American missionaries took baseball to Japan and British merchants introduced golf there. Skiing developed as a sport in Norway and became known in California by the 1860s.

No swords
British sailors brought judo back from Japan with them. It had been invented as a form of unarmed self-defence during a time when the samurai, the elite Japanese warrior class, were the only people allowed to carry swords.

Importing ideas
The British introduced cricket to India during colonization. It is now the national sport of India, Pakistan, Sri Lanka and Bangladesh.

The revived Olympics
The first modern Olympic Games were held in Athens in 1896. The Greek hosts fielded a team of 211 but the US, with only 14 people, won the most gold medals.

New ceremonies
Successive modern Games have added new symbols and ceremonies, such as the Olympic oath, flag and flame. The five rings on the Olympic flag represent the five continents of the world.

New events
The revived Olympics included ancient sports such as wrestling, running and throwing the javelin. But there were also new events such as shooting, fencing and cycling.

TIME OFF

Plantations

The spread of railways and steamships around the world made it possible to develop plantations which grew a single crop on a large scale to be sold to buyers far away. Caribbean islands specialized in sugar, which was also made into rum and molasses. The American South produced cotton, tobacco, rice and indigo. Tea and coffee were grown in the British colonies of India, Sri Lanka and Kenya for export. Farming had entered the era of globalization.

Black and white

On American plantations the black slaves lived in wooden shacks while the white owners lived in fine mansions. The division between rich white people and poor black people went on after slavery was ended.

Self-sufficiency
Many plantations grew much of their own food and had their own carpenters and blacksmiths to make or repair tools, buildings, wagons and furniture.

Demand for rubber
Rubber was originally tapped from trees growing wild in the Amazon forests of Brazil. Rubber plants were later taken to Malaya (Malaysia), where they are not naturally found. By laying out plantations, with plants in neat rows, it was possible to collect rubber far more efficiently than from plants growing scattered at random. Demand for rubber grew rapidly from the 1880s with the coming of bicycles and cars needing tyres, and electrical goods needing insulation.

Mass destruction

The history of warfare is the history of increasing firepower. In the American Civil War officers used revolvers which could fire five or six shots before they had to be reloaded. Single-shot muskets gave way to repeating rifles and machine-guns. In the 20th century the invention of aeroplanes brought aerial bombing which could destroy whole cities, killing and injuring civilians as well as enemy soldiers.

Treating casualties
Since the Korean War (1950–1953) helicopters have been taking the wounded swiftly from the battlefield to frontline surgery. In the past, severe wounds had often meant death from loss of blood, shock or cold.

World War I trenches
On the command of the whistle blast, soldiers had to leave their trench to dash across 'no man's land' towards enemy trenches. Few of the attackers survived.

Floating airbase

During World War II massive battles were fought between the US and Japanese navies in which the ships never saw each other but attacked using planes. Large scale warfare has come to involve less and less face-to-face combat.

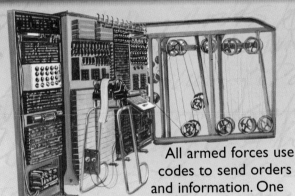

Breaking codes

At the press of a button

The age of nuclear warfare began in August 1945 with the dropping of a single atomic bomb on the Japanese city of Hiroshima and another on Nagasaki. Both cities were flattened and about 100,000 people in each city were killed instantly. Radiation sickness killed many more over following years. Today's nuclear weapons are hundreds of times more powerful and can be launched from submarines thousands of kilometres from their target.

All armed forces use codes to send orders and information. One aim of spying is to break these codes. During World War II the world's first programmable digital computer – Colossus (above) – was invented to break the complicated cipher produced by the Germans' brilliant Enigma machine.

Bullet Train

The world's first Bullet Train ran between the cities of Tokyo and Kyoto when Japan hosted the Olympics in 1964. It travelled at an average speed of 210 km/h and was a symbol of Japan's technological advances.

Global trade

By 1900 international trade had been revolutionized by fuel-efficient, steel-hulled steamships. Bulky goods, like timber could be carried cheaply over thousands of kilometres. The invention of refrigerator ships made it possible to bring meat half-way round the world from New Zealand to Britain. Aircraft travel was at first so expensive it could only be used for passengers and mail but nowadays is used even for fruit and flowers. The use of computer technology has led to globalization. The world is now a marketplace where information is traded as much as things.

Stock market
Dealers in stocks and shares, currencies and commodities used to work face-to-face. Nowadays most dealing is done on screens using information technology.

Global travel

The Wright brothers' first flight was less than the length of a jumbo jet. In 1909 Frenchman Louis Bleriot flew across the English Channel. In 1927 American Charles Lindbergh flew 4,830 km across the Atlantic alone. In 1961 Russian cosmonaut Yuri Gagarin became the first man to travel in space. US astronauts reached the Moon in 1969. Travel for ordinary people was revolutionized by cheap cars from the 1920s and cheap jet flights from the 1960s.

Passenger flight

A jumbo jet like the Boeing 747 carries over 400 passengers. By making long-haul flights cheaper, jumbo jets opened up Asia and Africa to tourism.

Travel in the future

Reusable US space shuttles point the way to interplanetary travel. But planes seem to have reached their technological limit with Concorde which is due to be phased out. New airbus designs stress larger passenger loads, greater passenger safety, more efficient use of fuels, less noise and less pollution. Travel by air is now often cheaper than travel by land.

First plane flight

The first manned, powered flights were made by Orville and Wilbur Wright at Kittyhawk, North Carolina in 1903. The very first flight lasted just 12 seconds.

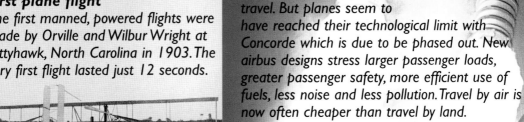

Dotcom City

As steam power died out, the typical industrial town was transformed. Jobs increasingly depended on communicating information, rather than making things. Many people now commute to an office but others are using computer technology to work at home. The home-workshop lifestyle of the days before the Industrial Revolution is being reinvented. Concern for conservation means that old and new buildings can exist side-by-side. Even modern steel frame buildings have designs influenced by classical architecture.

Instant communication

In the past, messenger-boys and postmen delivered information by hand. Computers, cables and satellites now link homes with each other and with massive stores of information via the Internet (left).

Cleaner living

Air pollution in cities now comes from vehicles rather than factories. As people move towards a cleaner environment we can expect a trend towards more pedestrian areas and bicycle lanes. In a world concerned with quality of life, people now demand that their towns be pleasant places in which to live.

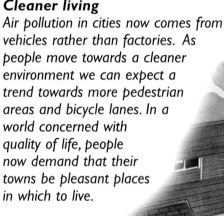

Many homes have satellite dishes

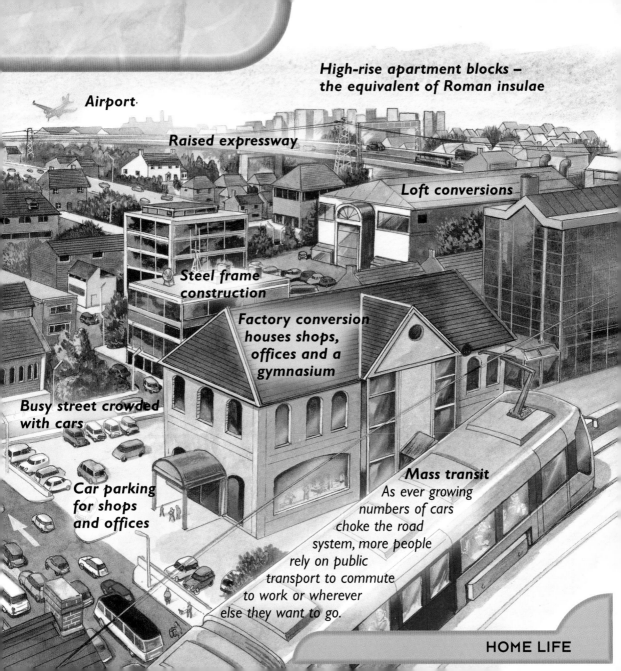

High-rise apartment blocks –
the equivalent of Roman insulae

Airport

Raised expressway

Loft conversions

Steel frame
construction

Factory conversion
houses shops,
offices and a
gymnasium

Busy street crowded
with cars

Car parking
for shops
and offices

Mass transit
As ever growing
numbers of cars
choke the road
system, more people
rely on public
transport to commute
to work or wherever
else they want to go.

Dictators and democrats

The history of the 20th century was dominated by struggles between democracies and dictatorships. Democracies like the USA and Britain have governments which can be changed by free elections. In a dictatorship there is usually only one political party – and power is controlled by its leader. The dictatorships that took over much of Europe in the 20th century have now been replaced by democracies. Some, like Denmark, Spain and Britain have an elected politician to run the country and a monarch for public ceremonies.

President Roosevelt

Franklin Delano Roosevelt (1882–1945) is the only person to have served as President of the United States four times. He is most famous for his policy called 'The New Deal' that led America out of the Great Depression in the 1930s.

Nelson Mandela

A fierce campaigner against South Africa's apartheid policies, Mandela spent 27 years in prison. In 1993 he won the Nobel Peace Prize. In 1994 he was elected President of South Africa in the country's first full democratic elections.

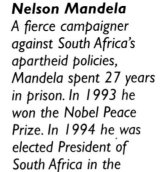

Lenin and Stalin

Vladimir Lenin (1870–1924, left) created the USSR as a Communist state. Joseph Stalin (1879–1953, right) ruled it as a brutal dictator. Both claimed to be building an ideal country for working people.

Changing faces

There have been four different portraits of the Queen shown on British coins since she took to the throne in 1953.

Hitler

The dictator, Adolf Hitler (1889–1945), came to power in Germany in 1933. His followers treated him as a political and military genius. His attempt to conquer Europe led to Germany's disastrous defeat in World War II. In the end, Hitler shot himself and Germany was divided into two countries for the next fifty years.

GLOSSARY

Afterlife A belief held by the ancient Egyptians that life continued after death.

Apartheid The South African policy of keeping different races of people apart (1949-1990).

Artillery Heavy long range guns.

Cavalry The part of an army that is made up of soldiers on horseback.

Civil war A war fought between groups of people from and in the same country or region.

Colonialism The policy of powerful nations which take control of areas controlled by weaker peoples.

Communism A form of government where the state owns all land and provides for people's needs.

Depression A period of severe decline in economic activity, causing widespread unemployment and hardship.

Democracy A form of government based on the rule of the people, usually through elected representatives.

Dictator A ruler with absolute power, usually unelected and ruling by force.

Empire A state and the conquered lands it rules over.

Famine A shortage of food often causing people to die of starvation.

Infantry The foot-soldiers of an army.

Myth An ancient traditional story of gods and heroes.

Nuclear Relating to or powered by the fission or fusion of atomic nuclei.

Parliament An assembly of the representatives (usually elected) of a group or nation.

Pollution Damage to the environment caused by human activity.

Protestantism A branch of the Christian Church that was started by Martin Luther in the 1500s.

Republic A state without a King or Queen, where the people elect their leader.

Sanitation Measures for the promotion of health and prevention of disease. Particularly drainage and sewage disposal.

Treaty An agreement between two or more parties.

INDEX